Book Report Instruction

You shouldn't do a book report on a book (unless instructed

Is less than 80 pages of writing
You have read before

<u>Your final book report can be handwritten in pencil, blue or black ink, or typed.</u>

Your report must include the following:

- Your name in the top right corner of the paper.

- The book's name, author, genre and publication date if applicable. (**Genre is essentially the type of book you're writing about. For example, such as "mystery" or "fantasy".**)

- At least 2-3 sentences describing the setting and or theme. (**Where and when the story took place.**)

- At least 2-3 sentences describing the main character(s). The main character in the book is also called the protagonist. The protagonist/main character is the person that the book is usually written about. (**You can describe things like their personality and or appearance.**)

- A paragraph (at least 5 sentences) detailing what happened in the beginning. (**What is the main character's conflict or problem?**)

- A paragraph (at least 5 sentences) detailing what happened in the middle. (**What did the character(s) do to solve the problem?**)

- A paragraph (at least 5 sentences) detailing what happened in the end. (**How was it finally resolved?**)

- Lastly, write at least 2-3 sentences stating your opinion about the book. Would you recommend this book?

Rate The Book ☆☆☆☆☆   **Today's Date** _____

Author _____

Book Title /Genre/Pub. Date _____

When and where does the story take place? _____

Identify and describe the main character. _____

OTHER CHARACTERS

What happened at the beginning? (What is the main character's conflict or problem?)	What happened at the end? (How was the problem finally resolved?)

What happened at the middle? (What did the character(s) do to solve the problem?)

Give your opinion of the book.

_____

_____

_____

Rate The Book ☆☆☆☆☆   **Today's Date** _____

Author _____

Book Title /Genre/Pub. Date _____

When and where does the story take place? _____

Identify and describe the main character. _____

OTHER CHARACTERS

| |
| |

What happened at the beginning? (What is the main character's conflict or problem?)

What happened at the end? (How was the problem finally resolved?)

What happened at the middle? (What did the character(s) do to solve the problem?)

Give your opinion of the book.

Rate The Book ☆☆☆☆☆   **Today's Date** _____

Author _____

Book Title /Genre/Pub. Date _____

When and where does the story take place? _____

Identify and describe the main character. _____

_____

OTHER CHARACTERS

What happened at the beginning? (What is the main character's conflict or problem?)	What happened at the end? (How was the problem finally resolved?)

What happened at the middle? (What did the character(s) do to solve the problem?)

Give your opinion of the book.

_____

_____

Rate The Book ☆ ☆ ☆ ☆ ☆   **Today's Date** _____

Author _____

Book Title /Genre/Pub. Date _____

When and where does the story take place? _____

Identify and describe the main character. _____

_____

OTHER CHARACTERS

What happened at the beginning? (What is the main character's conflict or problem?)

What happened at the end? (How was the problem finally resolved?)

What happened at the middle? (What did the character(s) do to solve the problem?)

Give your opinion of the book.

_____

_____

_____

Rate The Book ☆☆☆☆☆   **Today's Date** _____

Author _____

Book Title /Genre/Pub. Date _____

When and where does the story take place? _____

Identify and describe the main character. _____

OTHER CHARACTERS

What happened at the beginning? (What is the main character's conflict or problem?)	What happened at the end? (How was the problem finally resolved?)

What happened at the middle? (What did the character(s) do to solve the problem?)

Give your opinion of the book.

_____

_____

_____

Rate The Book ☆☆☆☆☆   **Today's Date** _____

Author _____

Book Title /Genre/Pub. Date _____

When and where does the story take place? _____

Identify and describe the main character. _____

OTHER CHARACTERS

What happened at the beginning? (What is the main character's conflict or problem?)

What happened at the end? (How was the problem finally resolved?)

What happened at the middle? (What did the character(s) do to solve the problem?)

Give your opinion of the book.

Rate The Book ☆☆☆☆☆   **Today's Date** _____

Author _____

Book Title /Genre/Pub. Date _____

When and where does the story take place? _____

Identify and describe the main character. _____

_____

OTHER CHARACTERS

What happened at the beginning? (What is the main character's conflict or problem?)

What happened at the end? (How was the problem finally resolved?)

What happened at the middle? (What did the character(s) do to solve the problem?)

Give your opinion of the book.

_____

_____

_____

Rate The Book ☆ ☆ ☆ ☆ ☆   **Today's Date** _____

Author _____

Book Title /Genre/Pub. Date _____

When and where does the story take place? _____

Identify and describe the main character. _____

_____

OTHER CHARACTERS

What happened at the beginning? (What is the main character's conflict or problem?)	What happened at the end? (How was the problem finally resolved?)

What happened at the middle? (What did the character(s) do to solve the problem?)	

Give your opinion of the book.

_____

_____

_____

Rate The Book ☆☆☆☆☆   **Today's Date** _____

Author _____

Book Title /Genre/Pub. Date _____

When and where does the story take place? _____

Identify and describe the main character. _____

_____

OTHER CHARACTERS

What happened at the beginning? (What is the main character's conflict or problem?)

What happened at the end? (How was the problem finally resolved?)

What happened at the middle? (What did the character(s) do to solve the problem?)

Give your opinion of the book.

Rate The Book ☆☆☆☆☆   **Today's Date** _____

Author _____

Book Title /Genre/Pub. Date _____

When and where does the story take place? _____

Identify and describe the main character. _____

OTHER CHARACTERS

What happened at the beginning? (What is the main character's conflict or problem?)

What happened at the end? (How was the problem finally resolved?)

What happened at the middle? (What did the character(s) do to solve the problem?)

Give your opinion of the book.

_____

_____

_____

Rate The Book ☆☆☆☆☆   **Today's Date** _____

Author _____

Book Title /Genre/Pub. Date _____

When and where does the story take place? _____

Identify and describe the main character. _____

_____

OTHER CHARACTERS

What happened at the beginning? (What is the main character's conflict or problem?)

What happened at the end? (How was the problem finally resolved?)

What happened at the middle? (What did the character(s) do to solve the problem?)

Give your opinion of the book.

_____

_____

_____

Rate The Book ☆☆☆☆☆   **Today's Date** _____

Author _____

Book Title /Genre/Pub. Date _____

When and where does the story take place? _____

Identify and describe the main character. _____

OTHER CHARACTERS

What happened at the beginning? (What is the main character's conflict or problem?)	What happened at the end? (How was the problem finally resolved?)

What happened at the middle? (What did the character(s) do to solve the problem?)

Give your opinion of the book.

_____

_____

_____

Rate The Book ☆☆☆☆☆   **Today's Date** _____

Author _____

Book Title /Genre/Pub. Date _____

When and where does the story take place? _____

Identify and describe the main character. _____

_____

OTHER CHARACTERS

What happened at the beginning? (What is the main character's conflict or problem?)

What happened at the end? (How was the problem finally resolved?)

What happened at the middle? (What did the character(s) do to solve the problem?)

Give your opinion of the book.

Rate The Book ☆☆☆☆☆   **Today's Date** _____

Author _____

Book Title /Genre/Pub. Date _____

When and where does the story take place? _____

Identify and describe the main character. _____

_____

OTHER CHARACTERS

What happened at the beginning? (What is the main character's conflict or problem?)

What happened at the end? (How was the problem finally resolved?)

What happened at the middle? (What did the character(s) do to solve the problem?)

Give your opinion of the book.

_____

_____

_____

Rate The Book ☆☆☆☆☆   **Today's Date** _____

Author _____

Book Title /Genre/Pub. Date _____

When and where does the story take place? _____

Identify and describe the main character. _____

_____

OTHER CHARACTERS

What happened at the beginning? (What is the main character's conflict or problem?)

What happened at the end? (How was the problem finally resolved?)

What happened at the middle? (What did the character(s) do to solve the problem?)

Give your opinion of the book.

_____

_____

_____

Rate The Book ☆☆☆☆☆   **Today's Date** _____

Author _____

Book Title /Genre/Pub. Date _____

When and where does the story take place? _____

Identify and describe the main character. _____

_____

OTHER CHARACTERS

[ ]

What happened at the beginning? (What is the main character's conflict or problem?)	What happened at the end? (How was the problem finally resolved?)

What happened at the middle? (What did the character(s) do to solve the problem?)

Give your opinion of the book.

_____

_____

_____

Rate The Book ☆☆☆☆☆   **Today's Date** _____

Author _____

Book Title /Genre/Pub. Date _____

When and where does the story take place? _____

Identify and describe the main character. _____

OTHER CHARACTERS

What happened at the beginning? (What is the main character's conflict or problem?)

What happened at the end? (How was the problem finally resolved?)

What happened at the middle? (What did the character(s) do to solve the problem?)

Give your opinion of the book.

_____

_____

Rate The Book ☆☆☆☆☆   **Today's Date** _____

Author _____

Book Title /Genre/Pub. Date _____

When and where does the story take place? _____

Identify and describe the main character. _____

_____

OTHER CHARACTERS

What happened at the beginning? (What is the main character's conflict or problem?)

What happened at the end? (How was the problem finally resolved?)

What happened at the middle? (What did the character(s) do to solve the problem?)

Give your opinion of the book.

_____

_____

_____

Rate The Book ☆☆☆☆☆   **Today's Date** _____

Author _____

Book Title /Genre/Pub. Date _____

When and where does the story take place? _____

Identify and describe the main character. _____

_____

OTHER CHARACTERS

What happened at the beginning? (What is the main character's conflict or problem?)	What happened at the end? (How was the problem finally resolved?)

What happened at the middle? (What did the character(s) do to solve the problem?)

Give your opinion of the book.

_____

_____

_____

Rate The Book ☆ ☆ ☆ ☆ ☆   **Today's Date** _____

Author _____

Book Title /Genre/Pub. Date _____

When and where does the story take place? _____

Identify and describe the main character. _____

_____

OTHER CHARACTERS

What happened at the beginning? (What is the main character's conflict or problem?)

What happened at the end? (How was the problem finally resolved?)

What happened at the middle? (What did the character(s) do to solve the problem?)

Give your opinion of the book.

_____

_____

_____

Rate The Book ☆☆☆☆☆   **Today's Date** _____

Author _____

Book Title /Genre/Pub. Date _____

When and where does the story take place? _____

Identify and describe the main character. _____

OTHER CHARACTERS

What happened at the beginning? (What is the main character's conflict or problem?)

What happened at the end? (How was the problem finally resolved?)

What happened at the middle? (What did the character(s) do to solve the problem?)

Give your opinion of the book.

_____

_____

_____

Rate The Book ☆☆☆☆☆   **Today's Date** _____

Author _____

Book Title /Genre/Pub. Date _____

When and where does the story take place? _____

Identify and describe the main character. _____

_____

OTHER CHARACTERS

What happened at the beginning? (What is the main character's conflict or problem?)	What happened at the end? (How was the problem finally resolved?)

What happened at the middle? (What did the character(s) do to solve the problem?)

Give your opinion of the book.

_____

_____

_____

Rate The Book ☆☆☆☆☆   **Today's Date** _____

Author _____

Book Title /Genre/Pub. Date _____

When and where does the story take place? _____

Identify and describe the main character. _____

_____

OTHER CHARACTERS

What happened at the beginning? (What is the main character's conflict or problem?)	What happened at the end? (How was the problem finally resolved?)

What happened at the middle? (What did the character(s) do to solve the problem?)

Give your opinion of the book.

_____

_____

_____

Rate The Book ☆☆☆☆☆   **Today's Date** _____

Author _____

Book Title /Genre/Pub. Date _____

When and where does the story take place? _____

Identify and describe the main character. _____

_____

OTHER CHARACTERS

What happened at the beginning? (What is the main character's conflict or problem?)

What happened at the end? (How was the problem finally resolved?)

What happened at the middle? (What did the character(s) do to solve the problem?)

Give your opinion of the book.

_____

_____

_____

Rate The Book ☆☆☆☆☆   **Today's Date** _____

Author _____

Book Title /Genre/Pub. Date _____

When and where does the story take place? _____

Identify and describe the main character. _____

_____

OTHER CHARACTERS

What happened at the beginning? (What is the main character's conflict or problem?)

What happened at the end? (How was the problem finally resolved?)

What happened at the middle? (What did the character(s) do to solve the problem?)

Give your opinion of the book.

_____

_____

_____

Rate The Book ☆☆☆☆☆   **Today's Date** _____

Author _____

Book Title /Genre/Pub. Date _____

When and where does the story take place?_____

Identify and describe the main character. _____

_____

OTHER CHARACTERS

What happened at the beginning? (What is the main character's conflict or problem?)	What happened at the end? (How was the problem finally resolved?)

What happened at the middle? (What did the character(s) do to solve the problem?)

Give your opinion of the book.

_____

_____

_____

Rate The Book ☆☆☆☆☆   **Today's Date** _____

Author _____

Book Title /Genre/Pub. Date _____

When and where does the story take place?_____

Identify and describe the main character. _____

_____

OTHER CHARACTERS

| |
| |

What happened at the beginning? (What is the main character's conflict or problem?)	What happened at the end? (How was the problem finally resolved?)

What happened at the middle? (What did the character(s) do to solve the problem?)

Give your opinion of the book.

_____

_____

_____

Rate The Book ☆ ☆ ☆ ☆ ☆   **Today's Date** _____

Author _____

Book Title /Genre/Pub. Date _____

When and where does the story take place? _____

Identify and describe the main character. _____

_____

OTHER CHARACTERS

What happened at the beginning? (What is the main character's conflict or problem?)	What happened at the end? (How was the problem finally resolved?)

What happened at the middle? (What did the character(s) do to solve the problem?)

Give your opinion of the book.

_____

_____

_____

Rate The Book ☆☆☆☆☆   **Today's Date** _____

Author _____

Book Title /Genre/Pub. Date _____

When and where does the story take place? _____

Identify and describe the main character. _____

_____

OTHER CHARACTERS

What happened at the beginning? (What is the main character's conflict or problem?)

What happened at the end? (How was the problem finally resolved?)

What happened at the middle? (What did the character(s) do to solve the problem?)

Give your opinion of the book.

_____

_____

_____

Rate The Book ☆☆☆☆☆   **Today's Date** _____

Author _____

Book Title /Genre/Pub. Date _____

When and where does the story take place? _____

Identify and describe the main character. _____

_____

OTHER CHARACTERS

| |
| |

What happened at the beginning? (What is the main character's conflict or problem?)	What happened at the end? (How was the problem finally resolved?)

What happened at the middle? (What did the character(s) do to solve the problem?)

Give your opinion of the book.

_____

_____

_____

Rate The Book ☆ ☆ ☆ ☆ ☆   **Today's Date** _____

Author _____

Book Title /Genre/Pub. Date _____

When and where does the story take place? _____

Identify and describe the main character. _____

_____

OTHER CHARACTERS

```
┌─────────────────────────────────────────────────────────┐
│                                                           │
│                                                           │
│                                                           │
│                                                           │
│                                                           │
└─────────────────────────────────────────────────────────┘
```

What happened at the beginning? (What is the main character's conflict or problem?)

_____

_____

_____

_____

_____

What happened at the end? (How was the problem finally resolved?)

_____

_____

_____

_____

_____

_____

_____

_____

_____

What happened at the middle? (What did the character(s) do to solve the problem?)

_____

_____

_____

_____

_____

Give your opinion of the book.

_____

_____

_____

Rate The Book ☆☆☆☆☆   **Today's Date** _____

Author _____

Book Title /Genre/Pub. Date _____

When and where does the story take place? _____

Identify and describe the main character. _____

_____

OTHER CHARACTERS

| |
| |

What happened at the beginning? (What is the main character's conflict or problem?)	What happened at the end? (How was the problem finally resolved?)

What happened at the middle? (What did the character(s) do to solve the problem?)

Give your opinion of the book.

_____

_____

_____

Rate The Book ☆☆☆☆☆   **Today's Date** _____

Author _____

Book Title /Genre/Pub. Date _____

When and where does the story take place? _____

Identify and describe the main character. _____

_____

OTHER CHARACTERS

What happened at the beginning? (What is the main character's conflict or problem?)	What happened at the end? (How was the problem finally resolved?)

What happened at the middle? (What did the character(s) do to solve the problem?)

Give your opinion of the book.

_____

_____

_____

Rate The Book ☆☆☆☆☆   **Today's Date** _____

Author _____

Book Title /Genre/Pub. Date _____

When and where does the story take place? _____

Identify and describe the main character. _____

_____

OTHER CHARACTERS

What happened at the beginning? (What is the main character's conflict or problem?)

What happened at the end? (How was the problem finally resolved?)

What happened at the middle? (What did the character(s) do to solve the problem?)

Give your opinion of the book.

_____

_____

_____

Rate The Book ☆☆☆☆☆   **Today's Date** _____

Author _____

Book Title /Genre/Pub. Date _____

When and where does the story take place? _____

Identify and describe the main character. _____

_____

OTHER CHARACTERS

What happened at the beginning? (What is the main character's conflict or problem?)	What happened at the end? (How was the problem finally resolved?)

What happened at the middle? (What did the character(s) do to solve the problem?)

Give your opinion of the book.

_____

_____

_____

Rate The Book ☆☆☆☆☆   **Today's Date** _____

Author _____

Book Title /Genre/Pub. Date _____

When and where does the story take place? _____

Identify and describe the main character. _____

_____

OTHER CHARACTERS

What happened at the beginning? (What is the main character's conflict or problem?)

What happened at the end? (How was the problem finally resolved?)

What happened at the middle? (What did the character(s) do to solve the problem?)

Give your opinion of the book.

_____

_____

_____

Rate The Book ☆☆☆☆☆ **Today's Date** _____

Author _____

Book Title /Genre/Pub. Date _____

When and where does the story take place? _____

Identify and describe the main character. _____

_____

OTHER CHARACTERS

What happened at the beginning? (What is the main character's conflict or problem?)	What happened at the end? (How was the problem finally resolved?)

What happened at the middle? (What did the character(s) do to solve the problem?)

Give your opinion of the book.

_____

_____

_____

Rate The Book ☆☆☆☆☆   **Today's Date** _____

Author _____

Book Title /Genre/Pub. Date _____

When and where does the story take place? _____

Identify and describe the main character. _____

OTHER CHARACTERS

What happened at the beginning? (What is the main character's conflict or problem?)

What happened at the end? (How was the problem finally resolved?)

What happened at the middle? (What did the character(s) do to solve the problem?)

Give your opinion of the book.

_____

_____

_____

Rate The Book ☆☆☆☆☆   **Today's Date** _____

Author _____

Book Title /Genre/Pub. Date _____

When and where does the story take place? _____

Identify and describe the main character. _____

_____

OTHER CHARACTERS

What happened at the beginning? (What is the main character's conflict or problem?)	What happened at the end? (How was the problem finally resolved?)

What happened at the middle? (What did the character(s) do to solve the problem?)

Give your opinion of the book.

_____

_____

_____

Rate The Book ☆☆☆☆☆   **Today's Date** _____

Author _____

Book Title /Genre/Pub. Date _____

When and where does the story take place? _____

Identify and describe the main character. _____

_____

OTHER CHARACTERS

| |
| |

What happened at the beginning? (What is the main character's conflict or problem?)	What happened at the end? (How was the problem finally resolved?)

What happened at the middle? (What did the character(s) do to solve the problem?)	

Give your opinion of the book.

_____

_____

_____

Rate The Book ☆☆☆☆☆   **Today's Date** _____

Author _____

Book Title /Genre/Pub. Date _____

When and where does the story take place?_____

Identify and describe the main character. _____

OTHER CHARACTERS

What happened at the beginning? (What is the main character's conflict or problem?)

What happened at the end? (How was the problem finally resolved?)

What happened at the middle? (What did the character(s) do to solve the problem?)

Give your opinion of the book.

_____

_____

_____

Rate The Book ☆☆☆☆☆   **Today's Date** _____

Author _____

Book Title /Genre/Pub. Date _____

When and where does the story take place? _____

Identify and describe the main character. _____

OTHER CHARACTERS

What happened at the beginning? (What is the main character's conflict or problem?)

What happened at the end? (How was the problem finally resolved?)

What happened at the middle? (What did the character(s) do to solve the problem?)

Give your opinion of the book.

Rate The Book ☆☆☆☆☆   **Today's Date** _____

Author _____

Book Title /Genre/Pub. Date _____

When and where does the story take place? _____

Identify and describe the main character. _____

_____

OTHER CHARACTERS

What happened at the beginning? (What is the main character's conflict or problem?)	What happened at the end? (How was the problem finally resolved?)

What happened at the middle? (What did the character(s) do to solve the problem?)

Give your opinion of the book.

_____

_____

_____

Rate The Book ☆☆☆☆☆   **Today's Date** _____

Author _____

Book Title /Genre/Pub. Date _____

When and where does the story take place? _____

Identify and describe the main character. _____

_____

OTHER CHARACTERS

What happened at the beginning? (What is the main character's conflict or problem?)	What happened at the end? (How was the problem finally resolved?)

What happened at the middle? (What did the character(s) do to solve the problem?)	

Give your opinion of the book.

_____

_____

_____

Rate The Book ☆☆☆☆☆　　**Today's Date** _____

Author _____

Book Title /Genre/Pub. Date _____

When and where does the story take place? _____

Identify and describe the main character. _____

_____

OTHER CHARACTERS

What happened at the beginning? (What is the main character's conflict or problem?)

What happened at the end? (How was the problem finally resolved?)

What happened at the middle? (What did the character(s) do to solve the problem?)

Give your opinion of the book.

_____

_____

_____

Rate The Book ☆☆☆☆☆   **Today's Date** _____

Author _____

Book Title /Genre/Pub. Date _____

When and where does the story take place? _____

Identify and describe the main character. _____

_____

OTHER CHARACTERS

What happened at the beginning? (What is the main character's conflict or problem?)	What happened at the end? (How was the problem finally resolved?)

What happened at the middle? (What did the character(s) do to solve the problem?)

Give your opinion of the book.

_____

_____

_____

Rate The Book ☆☆☆☆☆　　　**Today's Date** _____

Author _____

Book Title /Genre/Pub. Date _____

When and where does the story take place? _____

Identify and describe the main character. _____

_____

OTHER CHARACTERS

What happened at the beginning? (What is the main character's conflict or problem?)	What happened at the end? (How was the problem finally resolved?)

What happened at the middle? (What did the character(s) do to solve the problem?)

Give your opinion of the book.

_____

_____

_____

Rate The Book ☆☆☆☆☆   **Today's Date** _____

Author _____

Book Title /Genre/Pub. Date _____

When and where does the story take place? _____

Identify and describe the main character. _____

_____

OTHER CHARACTERS

What happened at the beginning? (What is the main character's conflict or problem?)	What happened at the end? (How was the problem finally resolved?)

What happened at the middle? (What did the character(s) do to solve the problem?)

Give your opinion of the book.

_____

_____

_____

Rate The Book ☆☆☆☆☆   **Today's Date** _____

Author _____

Book Title /Genre/Pub. Date _____

When and where does the story take place? _____

Identify and describe the main character. _____

_____

OTHER CHARACTERS

What happened at the beginning? (What is the main character's conflict or problem?)	What happened at the end? (How was the problem finally resolved?)

What happened at the middle? (What did the character(s) do to solve the problem?)

Give your opinion of the book.

_____

_____

_____

Rate The Book ☆☆☆☆☆   **Today's Date** _____

Author _____

Book Title /Genre/Pub. Date _____

When and where does the story take place? _____

Identify and describe the main character. _____

_____

OTHER CHARACTERS

What happened at the beginning? (What is the main character's conflict or problem?)	What happened at the end? (How was the problem finally resolved?)

What happened at the middle? (What did the character(s) do to solve the problem?)

Give your opinion of the book.

_____

_____

_____

Rate The Book ☆☆☆☆☆   **Today's Date** _____

Author _____

Book Title /Genre/Pub. Date _____

When and where does the story take place? _____

Identify and describe the main character. _____

_____

OTHER CHARACTERS

What happened at the beginning? (What is the main character's conflict or problem?)	What happened at the end? (How was the problem finally resolved?)

What happened at the middle? (What did the character(s) do to solve the problem?)

Give your opinion of the book.

_____

_____

_____

Rate The Book ☆☆☆☆☆   **Today's Date** _____

Author _____

Book Title /Genre/Pub. Date _____

When and where does the story take place? _____

Identify and describe the main character. _____

_____

OTHER CHARACTERS

What happened at the beginning? (What is the main character's conflict or problem?)	What happened at the end? (How was the problem finally resolved?)

What happened at the middle? (What did the character(s) do to solve the problem?)

Give your opinion of the book.

_____

_____

_____

Rate The Book ☆☆☆☆☆ **Today's Date** _____

Author _____

Book Title /Genre/Pub. Date _____

When and where does the story take place? _____

Identify and describe the main character. _____

OTHER CHARACTERS

What happened at the beginning? (What is the main character's conflict or problem?)

What happened at the end? (How was the problem finally resolved?)

What happened at the middle? (What did the character(s) do to solve the problem?)

Give your opinion of the book.

Rate The Book ☆ ☆ ☆ ☆ ☆   **Today's Date** _____

Author _____

Book Title /Genre/Pub. Date _____

When and where does the story take place? _____

Identify and describe the main character. _____
_____

OTHER CHARACTERS

[blank box]

What happened at the beginning? (What is the main character's conflict or problem?)

What happened at the end? (How was the problem finally resolved?)

What happened at the middle? (What did the character(s) do to solve the problem?)

Give your opinion of the book.

Rate The Book ☆☆☆☆☆   **Today's Date** _____

Author _____

Book Title /Genre/Pub. Date _____

When and where does the story take place?_____

Identify and describe the main character. _____

_____

OTHER CHARACTERS

What happened at the beginning? (What is the main character's conflict or problem?)

What happened at the end? (How was the problem finally resolved?)

What happened at the middle? (What did the character(s) do to solve the problem?)

Give your opinion of the book.

_____

_____

_____

Rate The Book ☆☆☆☆☆   **Today's Date** _____

Author _____

Book Title /Genre/Pub. Date _____

When and where does the story take place? _____

Identify and describe the main character. _____

_____

OTHER CHARACTERS

What happened at the beginning? (What is the main character's conflict or problem?)	What happened at the end? (How was the problem finally resolved?)

What happened at the middle? (What did the character(s) do to solve the problem?)	

Give your opinion of the book.

_____

_____

_____

Rate The Book ☆☆☆☆☆   **Today's Date** _____

Author _____

Book Title /Genre/Pub. Date _____

When and where does the story take place? _____

Identify and describe the main character. _____

_____

OTHER CHARACTERS

What happened at the beginning? (What is the main character's conflict or problem?)

What happened at the end? (How was the problem finally resolved?)

What happened at the middle? (What did the character(s) do to solve the problem?)

Give your opinion of the book.

_____

_____

_____

Rate The Book ☆ ☆ ☆ ☆ ☆   **Today's Date** _____

Author _____

Book Title /Genre/Pub. Date _____

When and where does the story take place? _____

Identify and describe the main character. _____

_____

OTHER CHARACTERS

What happened at the beginning? (What is the main character's conflict or problem?)	What happened at the end? (How was the problem finally resolved?)

What happened at the middle? (What did the character(s) do to solve the problem?)

Give your opinion of the book.

_____

_____

_____

Rate The Book ☆☆☆☆☆   **Today's Date** _____

Author _____

Book Title /Genre/Pub. Date _____

When and where does the story take place? _____

Identify and describe the main character. _____

_____

OTHER CHARACTERS

What happened at the beginning? (What is the main character's conflict or problem?)

What happened at the end? (How was the problem finally resolved?)

What happened at the middle? (What did the character(s) do to solve the problem?)

Give your opinion of the book.

_____

_____

_____

Rate The Book ☆☆☆☆☆   **Today's Date** _____

Author _____

Book Title /Genre/Pub. Date _____

When and where does the story take place? _____

Identify and describe the main character. _____

_____

OTHER CHARACTERS

What happened at the beginning? (What is the main character's conflict or problem?)	What happened at the end? (How was the problem finally resolved?)

What happened at the middle? (What did the character(s) do to solve the problem?)

Give your opinion of the book.

_____

_____

_____

Rate The Book ☆☆☆☆☆   **Today's Date** _____

Author _____

Book Title /Genre/Pub. Date _____

When and where does the story take place? _____

Identify and describe the main character. _____

_____

OTHER CHARACTERS

What happened at the beginning? (What is the main character's conflict or problem?)	What happened at the end? (How was the problem finally resolved?)

What happened at the middle? (What did the character(s) do to solve the problem?)

Give your opinion of the book.

_____

_____

Rate The Book ☆☆☆☆☆   **Today's Date** _____

Author _____

Book Title /Genre/Pub. Date _____

When and where does the story take place? _____

Identify and describe the main character. _____

OTHER CHARACTERS

What happened at the beginning? (What is the main character's conflict or problem?)	What happened at the end? (How was the problem finally resolved?)

What happened at the middle? (What did the character(s) do to solve the problem?)

Give your opinion of the book.

_____

_____

_____

Rate The Book ☆☆☆☆☆   **Today's Date** _____

Author _____

Book Title /Genre/Pub. Date _____

When and where does the story take place?_____

Identify and describe the main character. _____

_____

OTHER CHARACTERS

What happened at the beginning? (What is the main character's conflict or problem?)	What happened at the end? (How was the problem finally resolved?)

What happened at the middle? (What did the character(s) do to solve the problem?)

Give your opinion of the book.

_____

_____

_____

Rate The Book ☆☆☆☆☆   **Today's Date** _____

Author _____

Book Title /Genre/Pub. Date _____

When and where does the story take place? _____

Identify and describe the main character. _____

_____

OTHER CHARACTERS

What happened at the beginning? (What is the main character's conflict or problem?)	What happened at the end? (How was the problem finally resolved?)

What happened at the middle? (What did the character(s) do to solve the problem?)

Give your opinion of the book.

_____

_____

_____

Rate The Book ☆☆☆☆☆   **Today's Date** _____

Author _____

Book Title /Genre/Pub. Date _____

When and where does the story take place? _____

Identify and describe the main character. _____

_____

OTHER CHARACTERS

What happened at the beginning? (What is the main character's conflict or problem?)

What happened at the end? (How was the problem finally resolved?)

What happened at the middle? (What did the character(s) do to solve the problem?)

Give your opinion of the book.

_____

_____

_____

Rate The Book ☆☆☆☆☆   **Today's Date** _____

Author _____

Book Title /Genre/Pub. Date _____

When and where does the story take place? _____

Identify and describe the main character. _____

OTHER CHARACTERS

What happened at the beginning? (What is the main character's conflict or problem?)	What happened at the end? (How was the problem finally resolved?)

What happened at the middle? (What did the character(s) do to solve the problem?)

Give your opinion of the book.

Rate The Book ☆☆☆☆☆   **Today's Date** _____

Author _____

Book Title /Genre/Pub. Date _____

When and where does the story take place? _____

Identify and describe the main character. _____

OTHER CHARACTERS

| |
| |

What happened at the beginning? (What is the main character's conflict or problem?)

What happened at the end? (How was the problem finally resolved?)

What happened at the middle? (What did the character(s) do to solve the problem?)

Give your opinion of the book.

_____

_____

_____

Rate The Book ☆☆☆☆☆   **Today's Date** _____

Author _____

Book Title /Genre/Pub. Date _____

When and where does the story take place? _____

Identify and describe the main character. _____

_____

OTHER CHARACTERS

What happened at the beginning? (What is the main character's conflict or problem?)	What happened at the end? (How was the problem finally resolved?)

What happened at the middle? (What did the character(s) do to solve the problem?)	

Give your opinion of the book.

_____

_____

_____

Rate The Book ☆☆☆☆☆   **Today's Date** _____

Author _____

Book Title /Genre/Pub. Date _____

When and where does the story take place? _____

Identify and describe the main character. _____

_____

OTHER CHARACTERS

What happened at the beginning? (What is the main character's conflict or problem?)	What happened at the end? (How was the problem finally resolved?)

What happened at the middle? (What did the character(s) do to solve the problem?)

Give your opinion of the book.

_____

_____

Rate The Book ☆☆☆☆☆   **Today's Date** _____

Author _____

Book Title /Genre/Pub. Date _____

When and where does the story take place?_____

Identify and describe the main character. _____

_____

OTHER CHARACTERS

What happened at the beginning? (What is the main character's conflict or problem?)	What happened at the end? (How was the problem finally resolved?)

What happened at the middle? (What did the character(s) do to solve the problem?)

Give your opinion of the book.

_____

_____

_____

Rate The Book ☆☆☆☆☆   **Today's Date** _____

Author _____

Book Title /Genre/Pub. Date _____

When and where does the story take place? _____

Identify and describe the main character. _____

_____

OTHER CHARACTERS

What happened at the beginning? (What is the main character's conflict or problem?)	What happened at the end? (How was the problem finally resolved?)

What happened at the middle? (What did the character(s) do to solve the problem?)

Give your opinion of the book.

_____

_____

_____

Rate The Book ☆☆☆☆☆   **Today's Date** _____

Author _____

Book Title /Genre/Pub. Date _____

When and where does the story take place? _____

Identify and describe the main character. _____

_____

OTHER CHARACTERS

What happened at the beginning? (What is the main character's conflict or problem?)	What happened at the end? (How was the problem finally resolved?)

What happened at the middle? (What did the character(s) do to solve the problem?)

Give your opinion of the book.

_____

_____

_____

Rate The Book ☆☆☆☆☆   **Today's Date** _____

Author _____

Book Title /Genre/Pub. Date _____

When and where does the story take place? _____

Identify and describe the main character. _____

_____

OTHER CHARACTERS

What happened at the beginning? (What is the main character's conflict or problem?)

What happened at the end? (How was the problem finally resolved?)

What happened at the middle? (What did the character(s) do to solve the problem?)

Give your opinion of the book.

Rate The Book ☆☆☆☆☆   **Today's Date** _____

Author _____

Book Title /Genre/Pub. Date _____

When and where does the story take place? _____

Identify and describe the main character. _____

OTHER CHARACTERS

| |
| |

| What happened at the beginning? (What is the main character's conflict or problem?) | What happened at the end? (How was the problem finally resolved?) |

| What happened at the middle? (What did the character(s) do to solve the problem?) | |

Give your opinion of the book.

_____

_____

_____

Rate The Book ☆☆☆☆☆   **Today's Date** _____

Author _____

Book Title /Genre/Pub. Date _____

When and where does the story take place? _____

Identify and describe the main character. _____

OTHER CHARACTERS

What happened at the beginning? (What is the main character's conflict or problem?)

What happened at the end? (How was the problem finally resolved?)

What happened at the middle? (What did the character(s) do to solve the problem?)

Give your opinion of the book.

Rate The Book ☆☆☆☆☆   **Today's Date** _____

Author _____

Book Title /Genre/Pub. Date _____

When and where does the story take place? _____

Identify and describe the main character. _____

_____

OTHER CHARACTERS

| |
| |

What happened at the beginning? (What is the main character's conflict or problem?)	What happened at the end? (How was the problem finally resolved?)

What happened at the middle? (What did the character(s) do to solve the problem?)

Give your opinion of the book.

_____

_____

_____

Rate The Book ☆☆☆☆☆   **Today's Date** _____

Author _____

Book Title /Genre/Pub. Date _____

When and where does the story take place? _____

Identify and describe the main character. _____

_____

OTHER CHARACTERS

What happened at the beginning? (What is the main character's conflict or problem?)	What happened at the end? (How was the problem finally resolved?)

What happened at the middle? (What did the character(s) do to solve the problem?)

Give your opinion of the book.

_____

_____

Rate The Book ☆☆☆☆☆   **Today's Date** _____

Author _____

Book Title /Genre/Pub. Date _____

When and where does the story take place? _____

Identify and describe the main character. _____

OTHER CHARACTERS

What happened at the beginning? (What is the main character's conflict or problem?)	What happened at the end? (How was the problem finally resolved?)

What happened at the middle? (What did the character(s) do to solve the problem?)

Give your opinion of the book.

_____

_____

_____

Rate The Book ☆☆☆☆☆   **Today's Date** _____

Author _____

Book Title /Genre/Pub. Date _____

When and where does the story take place? _____

Identify and describe the main character. _____

_____

OTHER CHARACTERS

What happened at the beginning? (What is the main character's conflict or problem?)	What happened at the end? (How was the problem finally resolved?)

What happened at the middle? (What did the character(s) do to solve the problem?)

Give your opinion of the book.

_____

_____

_____

Rate The Book ☆☆☆☆☆   **Today's Date** _____

Author _____

Book Title /Genre/Pub. Date _____

When and where does the story take place? _____

Identify and describe the main character. _____

_____

OTHER CHARACTERS

What happened at the beginning? (What is the main character's conflict or problem?)	What happened at the end? (How was the problem finally resolved?)

What happened at the middle? (What did the character(s) do to solve the problem?)

Give your opinion of the book.

_____

_____

_____

Rate The Book ☆☆☆☆☆   **Today's Date** _____

Author _____

Book Title /Genre/Pub. Date _____

When and where does the story take place? _____

Identify and describe the main character. _____

OTHER CHARACTERS

What happened at the beginning? (What is the main character's conflict or problem?)	What happened at the end? (How was the problem finally resolved?)

What happened at the middle? (What did the character(s) do to solve the problem?)

Give your opinion of the book.

Rate The Book ☆ ☆ ☆ ☆ ☆   **Today's Date** _____

Author _____

Book Title /Genre/Pub. Date _____

When and where does the story take place? _____

Identify and describe the main character. _____

_____

OTHER CHARACTERS

What happened at the beginning? (What is the main character's conflict or problem?)	What happened at the end? (How was the problem finally resolved?)

What happened at the middle? (What did the character(s) do to solve the problem?)

Give your opinion of the book.

_____

_____

_____

Rate The Book ☆☆☆☆☆   **Today's Date** _____

Author _____

Book Title /Genre/Pub. Date _____

When and where does the story take place? _____

Identify and describe the main character. _____

OTHER CHARACTERS

What happened at the beginning? (What is the main character's conflict or problem?)

What happened at the end? (How was the problem finally resolved?)

What happened at the middle? (What did the character(s) do to solve the problem?)

Give your opinion of the book.

_____

_____

_____

Rate The Book ☆☆☆☆☆   **Today's Date** _____

Author _____

Book Title /Genre/Pub. Date _____

When and where does the story take place? _____

Identify and describe the main character. _____

_____

OTHER CHARACTERS

| |
| |

What happened at the beginning? (What is the main character's conflict or problem?)	What happened at the end? (How was the problem finally resolved?)

What happened at the middle? (What did the character(s) do to solve the problem?)

Give your opinion of the book.

_____

_____

_____

Rate The Book ☆☆☆☆☆   **Today's Date** _____

Author _____

Book Title /Genre/Pub. Date _____

When and where does the story take place? _____

Identify and describe the main character. _____

OTHER CHARACTERS

What happened at the beginning? (What is the main character's conflict or problem?)

What happened at the end? (How was the problem finally resolved?)

What happened at the middle? (What did the character(s) do to solve the problem?)

Give your opinion of the book.

Rate The Book ☆☆☆☆☆   **Today's Date** _____

Author _____

Book Title /Genre/Pub. Date _____

When and where does the story take place? _____

Identify and describe the main character. _____

OTHER CHARACTERS

What happened at the beginning? (What is the main character's conflict or problem?)

What happened at the end? (How was the problem finally resolved?)

What happened at the middle? (What did the character(s) do to solve the problem?)

Give your opinion of the book.

Rate The Book ☆☆☆☆☆   **Today's Date** _____

Author _____

Book Title /Genre/Pub. Date _____

When and where does the story take place? _____

Identify and describe the main character. _____

_____

OTHER CHARACTERS

What happened at the beginning? (What is the main character's conflict or problem?)	What happened at the end? (How was the problem finally resolved?)

What happened at the middle? (What did the character(s) do to solve the problem?)

Give your opinion of the book.

_____

_____

_____

Rate The Book ☆☆☆☆☆　　**Today's Date** _____

Author _____

Book Title /Genre/Pub. Date _____

When and where does the story take place? _____

Identify and describe the main character. _____

_____

OTHER CHARACTERS

What happened at the beginning? (What is the main character's conflict or problem?)	What happened at the end? (How was the problem finally resolved?)

What happened at the middle? (What did the character(s) do to solve the problem?)

Give your opinion of the book.

_____

_____

_____

Rate The Book ☆☆☆☆☆   **Today's Date** _____

Author _____

Book Title /Genre/Pub. Date _____

When and where does the story take place? _____

Identify and describe the main character. _____

_____

OTHER CHARACTERS

What happened at the beginning? (What is the main character's conflict or problem?)	What happened at the end? (How was the problem finally resolved?)

What happened at the middle? (What did the character(s) do to solve the problem?)

Give your opinion of the book.

_____

_____

_____

Rate The Book ☆☆☆☆☆   **Today's Date** _____

Author _____

Book Title /Genre/Pub. Date _____

When and where does the story take place? _____

Identify and describe the main character. _____

OTHER CHARACTERS

| |
| |

What happened at the beginning? (What is the main character's conflict or problem?)	What happened at the end? (How was the problem finally resolved?)

What happened at the middle? (What did the character(s) do to solve the problem?)

Give your opinion of the book.

_____

_____

_____

Rate The Book ☆☆☆☆☆   **Today's Date** _____

Author _____

Book Title /Genre/Pub. Date _____

When and where does the story take place? _____

Identify and describe the main character. _____

_____

OTHER CHARACTERS

What happened at the beginning? (What is the main character's conflict or problem?)

What happened at the end? (How was the problem finally resolved?)

What happened at the middle? (What did the character(s) do to solve the problem?)

Give your opinion of the book.

_____

_____

_____

Rate The Book ☆☆☆☆☆   **Today's Date** _____

Author _____

Book Title /Genre/Pub. Date _____

When and where does the story take place? _____

Identify and describe the main character. _____

_____

OTHER CHARACTERS

What happened at the beginning? (What is the main character's conflict or problem?)	What happened at the end? (How was the problem finally resolved?)

What happened at the middle? (What did the character(s) do to solve the problem?)

Give your opinion of the book.

_____

_____

Rate The Book ☆☆☆☆☆   **Today's Date** _____

Author _____

Book Title /Genre/Pub. Date _____

When and where does the story take place? _____

Identify and describe the main character. _____

OTHER CHARACTERS

What happened at the beginning? (What is the main character's conflict or problem?)

What happened at the end? (How was the problem finally resolved?)

What happened at the middle? (What did the character(s) do to solve the problem?)

Give your opinion of the book.

_____

_____

_____

Rate The Book ☆☆☆☆☆   **Today's Date** _____

Author _____

Book Title /Genre/Pub. Date _____

When and where does the story take place? _____

Identify and describe the main character. _____

OTHER CHARACTERS

What happened at the beginning? (What is the main character's conflict or problem?)

What happened at the end? (How was the problem finally resolved?)

What happened at the middle? (What did the character(s) do to solve the problem?)

Give your opinion of the book.

_____

_____

_____

Rate The Book ☆☆☆☆☆   **Today's Date** _____

Author _____

Book Title /Genre/Pub. Date _____

When and where does the story take place? _____

Identify and describe the main character. _____

_____

OTHER CHARACTERS

What happened at the beginning? (What is the main character's conflict or problem?)

What happened at the end? (How was the problem finally resolved?)

What happened at the middle? (What did the character(s) do to solve the problem?)

Give your opinion of the book.

Rate The Book ☆☆☆☆☆   **Today's Date** _____

Author _____

Book Title /Genre/Pub. Date _____

When and where does the story take place? _____

Identify and describe the main character. _____

_____

OTHER CHARACTERS

_____

| What happened at the beginning? (What is the main character's conflict or problem?) | What happened at the end? (How was the problem finally resolved?) |

What happened at the middle? (What did the character(s) do to solve the problem?)

Give your opinion of the book.

Rate The Book ☆☆☆☆☆   **Today's Date** _____

Author _____

Book Title /Genre/Pub. Date _____

When and where does the story take place? _____

Identify and describe the main character. _____

OTHER CHARACTERS

What happened at the beginning? (What is the main character's conflict or problem?)	What happened at the end? (How was the problem finally resolved?)

What happened at the middle? (What did the character(s) do to solve the problem?)

Give your opinion of the book.

_____

_____

_____

Rate The Book ☆☆☆☆☆   **Today's Date** _____

Author _____

Book Title /Genre/Pub. Date _____

When and where does the story take place? _____

Identify and describe the main character. _____

OTHER CHARACTERS

What happened at the beginning? (What is the main character's conflict or problem?)

What happened at the end? (How was the problem finally resolved?)

What happened at the middle? (What did the character(s) do to solve the problem?)

Give your opinion of the book.

Rate The Book ☆☆☆☆☆   **Today's Date** _____

Author _____

Book Title /Genre/Pub. Date _____

When and where does the story take place? _____

Identify and describe the main character. _____

_____

OTHER CHARACTERS

What happened at the beginning? (What is the main character's conflict or problem?)

What happened at the end? (How was the problem finally resolved?)

What happened at the middle? (What did the character(s) do to solve the problem?)

Give your opinion of the book.

_____

_____

_____

My Planner

○ MONDAY

PRIORITIES

_____

_____

○ TUESDAY

_____

_____

_____

○ WEDNESDAY

TO DO

_____

_____

○ THURSDAY

_____

_____

_____

_____

○ FRIDAY

_____

_____

_____

○ SATURDAY / SUNDAY

_____

_____

My Planner

○ MONDAY

PRIORITIES

_____

○ TUESDAY

_____

_____

_____

○ WEDNESDAY

_____

TO DO

_____

○ THURSDAY

_____

_____

_____

○ FRIDAY

_____

_____

_____

○ SATURDAY / SUNDAY

_____

_____

My Planner

○ MONDAY

PRIORITIES

○ TUESDAY

○ WEDNESDAY

TO DO

○ THURSDAY

○ FRIDAY

○ SATURDAY / SUNDAY

My Planner

○ MONDAY

PRIORITIES

○ TUESDAY

○ WEDNESDAY

TO DO

○ THURSDAY

○ FRIDAY

○ SATURDAY / SUNDAY

My Planner

○ MONDAY

PRIORITIES

_____

_____

○ TUESDAY

_____

_____

_____

_____

○ WEDNESDAY

TO DO

_____

○ THURSDAY

_____

_____

_____

_____

○ FRIDAY

_____

_____

_____

○ SATURDAY / SUNDAY

_____

_____

My Planner

○ MONDAY

                                                PRIORITIES

○ TUESDAY

○ WEDNESDAY

                                                TO DO

○ THURSDAY

○ FRIDAY

○ SATURDAY / SUNDAY

My Planner

○ MONDAY

PRIORITIES

○ TUESDAY

○ WEDNESDAY

TO DO

○ THURSDAY

○ FRIDAY

○ SATURDAY / SUNDAY

MY GRADES TRACKER

Week	Monday	Tuesday	Wednesday	Thursday	Friday
1					
2					
3					
4					
5					
6					
7					
8					
9					
10					
11					
12					
13					
14					
15					
16					
17					
18					

Notes

MY GRADES TRACKER

Week	Monday	Tuesday	Wednesday	Thursday	Friday
1					
2					
3					
4					
5					
6					
7					
8					
9					
10					
11					
12					
13					
14					
15					
16					
17					
18					

Notes

Made in the USA
Las Vegas, NV
20 January 2024

84464840R10063